WHERE ETERNITY IS LEARNED

OTHER BOOKS AND CHAPBOOKS BY ADELE KENNY

POETRY
Wind Over Stones
Not Asking What If
A Lightness, A Thirst, or Nothing at All
What Matters
The Kite & Other Poems from Childhood
Chosen Ghosts
Illegal Entries
An Archaeology of Ruins
At the Edge of the Woods
Starship Earth
Castles and Dragons
Questi Momenti
Migrating Geese
Between Hail Marys
The Roses Open
Notes from the Nursing Home

NONFICTION
Chapbooks: A Historical Perspective
Staffordshire Figures: History in Earthenware 1740–1900
Photographic Cases: Victorian Design Sources 1840–1870
Staffordshire Animals: A Collector's Guide
Staffordshire Spaniels: A Collector's Guide
We Become By Being
The Silence and the Flame: Clare and Francis of Assisi
Counseling Gifted, Creative, and Talented Youth
    Through the Arts
A Creative Writing Companion

WHERE ETERNITY IS LEARNED

Adele Kenny

Welcome Rain Publishers
NEW YORK

Pages 67–69 contain credits for previously published poems.

Welcome Rain
215 Thompson Street #473
New York, New York 10012

www.welcomerain.com

ISBN: 978-1-56649-433-5

Book design by Smythtype Design
Jacket image: Ángeles Santos
Celestial Harmony (Armonia celeste), 1929
Reina Sofia Museum, Madrid
Photo Credit: Album/Art Resource, NY

In Loving Memory of
Rev. Alex D. Pinto
(December 24, 1944–September 7, 2023)

ॐ

Anam Cara—Soul Friend
gone to the place where eternity is learned.

...the end of all our exploring
Will be to arrive where we started
And know the place for the first time.

—T.S. ELIOT (from "Little Gidding")

CONTENTS

I

II

III

I

&

There is always one moment in childhood
when the door opens and lets the future in.

—Graham Greene

The Old House

The house my great-uncle built
is a cinderblock bag of cracked ceilings

and long windows.

Smaller than memory believes, this is
the front porch place of my childhood—

old furniture fortress of windy nights

in an attic bedroom where closet curtains
kept me awake because they moved. This is

the family house where my mother

came into the world and left it, where four
generations of family members spent their lives.

Tonight, a broken window blinks back

the moon. Leaves move in the star-driven
dark, and the sound echoes lightly

as if someone is whispering my name.

On Summer Nights

Sometimes, on summer nights (after an early bath and dressed in pajamas), my parents took me to a drive-in theater where the moon, high above the biggest screen I'd ever seen, beamed down on rows of cars, arranged in their spaces like lines on a ruler.

I saw *Davy Crockett* and *Cinderella* there, but the drive-in became a marginal joy the night I saw *Old Yeller*—the gunshot, the dog's still body—and I felt for the first time what I would later call sorrow. All the way home I struggled with fear for my own dog (Missy) who would die the night I graduated from high school. But that was the future, and I'd just learned that we lose what we love.

That Little While...

We needed a priest or a monk to play the game, so we
shot odds and evens for the role, and I won. The only kid
on the block who wasn't Catholic, I needed a name and
thought of Friar Tuck, but *Tuck* was too close to that

forbidden word we used when our parents weren't around.
So they called me *Fr. Percival*, a name lifted from
the Roundtable in a mixed metaphor of fiction and faith.
We lived in a place where difference didn't matter—

not gender, not color, not even belief—we were all the
same in our differences. Dressed in my mother's brown
bathrobe (a jump rope tied at my waist), I lined the kids up
on Saturday mornings, lifted my arms, and chanted *Dominus*

vo-bi-scum (as monk-like as possible). I had no idea what that
meant, but the kids told me to say it, so I did. And then,
Communion—Necco wafers—round, flat candies—every flavor
except licorice (which *we* believed was the devil's favorite).

But, the Catholic kids said they needed confession before
communion. Not something we did in *my* church—as
mysterious to me as Latin—I sat in Mrs. Malone's refrigerator
crate with a piece of old curtain (just sheer enough to

see through) between the penitents and me. One by one,
they came to our ritual telling, and I doled out penances
as simple as their sins—reasonably easy until Anthony
claimed that he coveted Maureen's ass. Bowing his head

on the other side of the curtain, he said (in a voice too
small for his usual bravado) that he knocked Maureen
on her butt because he felt like it. A nun had told him
Thou shalt not covet thy neighbor's ass, and because

he pushed Maureen onto hers, he was sure that he
coveted. Clueless, I had no idea what *coveted* meant,
but he said he was sorry, so I told him to stand in
the woods across the street (all by himself) and to sing

"Onward Christian Soldiers." Already humbled by the
things we didn't have and where we lived (on the wrong
side of Route 1), we made life up as we went along.
We were shabby and poor, but we knew who we were.

Completely certain there were spirits in the woods where
Anthony sang alone, we went from our "church" into
that deeper green to find them. If I listen softly, I can
almost hear us shuffle through leaves on the dirt path.

In our old neighborhood, above the battered sidewalks, and
the storm sewer that overflowed when it rained, saints
sat high inside their heaven. Sparrows and crows defined
the sky. In those days, before we knew how fleeting

childhood would be, how memory would become a dog
that howls backwards—before we saw those days in grayscale
or understood our own sadness—something holy called
us to itself and held us there for just that little while.

One of Us

His name was Richard, and he was one of us, a
neighborhood kid who lived in one of the tired
houses on the other side of Route 1, a place
where trucks rumbled through dreams, and
small planes from Linden Airport flew overhead.

Separated from the rest of Rahway by the highway's
paved line, safe inside our thin streets and broken
sidewalks, we played together at Flanagan's Field.
All equally poor—equally the same—we had no
idea that people lived differently in other parts of town.

In the early 50s, "gym" wasn't a regular subject,
but once a week we first graders put on our sneakers
and went to that huge room overhung with basketball
nets and lined with bleachers. There, our teacher
marched us in tight formation, in staggered ranks,

in moving circles. One week, she told the girls
to choose partners for folk dancing. Of course, I
chose Richard—he was my friend—and what fun
it was to spin around the gym in our own versions
of the tarantella, the polka, the Irish jig.

That afternoon, on the playground, I found Richard
hunched by a row of hedges. He was crying, but
when I went to him, he shrugged me away and
covered his face with his hands. It was then that
a group of kids made a circle around me and

chanted, *n----r lover, n----r lover.* Strangely afraid,
I ran from the schoolyard and crossed Route 1 by
myself (something I was forbidden to do). My
parents must have contacted the school because
the taunting stopped, but something innocent

changed that day. Richard and I stayed friends until
high school when his family moved away. I didn't
see him again until years later in a local ShopRite.
I heard a voice say my name, I turned, and there
was Richard. We spoke for a while about who we

had become and, then, he bowed from the waist and
smiled. I curtseyed, and there we were doing a crazy
waltz down the produce aisle, past canned goods
and candies, past a dozen shoppers who stepped back
and, watching us, slowly began to applaud.

Things You're Told

*You better watch out, / You better not cry, / Better not pout, /
I'm telling you why: /Santa Claus is comin' to town. /
He's making a list / And checking it twice, / Gonna find out /
Who's naughty and nice. / Santa Claus is comin' to town.*
                    (From "Santa Claus Is Comin' to Town"
                        by J. Fred Coots and Haven Gillespie)

It's funny how things you're told as a child stay
with you, how certain people get into your head
and never leave. I had an aunt who did that.
When she walked me to school, she whipped
my legs with a willow stick because I cried and
didn't want to go. She told me I was bad, that God

kept a book in which he recorded every time I
misbehaved. She said that God and Santa worked
together; and, just like God, Santa kept a list of
all the naughty things I did. In the time between
one Christmas and another, he marked that list
and checked it twice (just as the song said).

That year, my parents took me to Bamberger's
where I sat on Santa's lap. Too terrified to cry,
I could only stare at him, speechless. Someone
took a picture, and there I am, forever held in
sepia fright. I was sure I was doomed—my aunt
said the marks beneath my name were forever.

I imagined them unmovable as the stones that
lined our driveway, and me with no way to lift
myself above them. When the snow came that
winter, it covered everything, including the driveway
stones I knew were still there. That Christmas Eve
I shivered into sleep, expecting nothing.

Exactly Then

The "wolf hat" came from a church rummage sale—tattered and ratty—not real fur, but the color reminded me of wolf pictures I saved from an old *Geographic*. I must have been seven or eight with just enough change in my pocket to buy it.

Back then, across the street from our house, were acres of woods—a forbidden place where my mother said creatures fed on children and fear. But years before I learned how to be afraid, the distant mystery of that forest called to me, and I went to its wildness when everyone else was asleep.

One night, curled into a pile of fallen leaves—"wolf hat" on—I pretended (without purpose or understanding) that I *was* a wolf. As I moved into the trees' silence, nothing was real but that moment (nothing before or after—no thought to consequence, how things unwind). There was only *exactly then* and a spirit fluent inside me. Under the stars' stretched brilliance, it was as if I truly became something other. Moonlight blew through me and became the wind—the small wild song that I was.

Time Warp

With a bit of a mind flip—You're into the time slip—
And nothing can ever be the same...
            (From "The Time Warp," *The Rocky Horror Picture Show*)

Back then, it was just for fun (the midnight movie seen over
and over)—costumes and props—a candle on Venus de Milo's
head. Ridiculous really, and no context for it now—a Gothic
spoof, a group of friends shouting out dialogue, water pistols
ready to soak anyone close when Janet and Brad walked into
the storm.

Happier companions than we would have been in our own
thoughts, we tossed confetti like shredded love letters, snapped
our rubber gloves with Frank, and threw toilet tissue into the
air when Brad cried out, *Great Scott!*

Most of those friends disappeared years ago and only come
back as unintentional memories, held in a time warp where
young was simply young, and nothing can ever be the same.

Of Shadows

The Ginny doll arrived in November for
my seventh birthday. All my friends had
Ginny dolls, complete with clothes and
furniture. I hoped Santa would bring my
doll the same. But what I found under
the tree was Ginny-sized furniture that
my father made (long nights while I slept).
Crafted from pine and upholstered—not
real Ginny furniture—homemade pieces I
was too embarrassed to show my friends.

Years later, long after my parents were
gone, I found Ginny and her furniture
in the cellar of our old house, carefully
packed with a note in my mother's
handwriting: *I thought you might want
these someday.* I brought them here to
this house, recovered the sofa and chair,
and restored Ginny's hair to match my own.

Ginny lives in my library now, in a glass
case with the furniture my father made.
She stands between a small table and an
armoire that only holds a single change of
clothes. There are times I wish I lived there
too. Looking through glass from the inside
out, I'd curl into Ginny's chair and tell her
about the perfection of shadows—how
memory is a cypher, a code that takes us
back to all that, later, becomes important.

Anything with Wings

The day I sold our family house,
I closed and locked the door and

never went back. Never curious
to see what the new owner would

do with the only home of my
childhood, I have no idea what

happened to it, no idea if anything
was left in some dark corner or on

the hidden staircase closed off in
the emptiness of my mother's closet.

That life, as I knew it, was gone
years before I let it go—a stippled

history of secrets and sadness—
dreams that lingered but couldn't

come true. As a child inside that
past, I believed in anything with

wings—haloed angels, birds with
feathers like crested sunlight,

and moths that fluttered dust on
my hands when I touched them.

In the woods across the street (by the
pond where wild ducks came each

autumn), my cousin Eddie found a space
where heaven's light sifted through

darkness and traced our faces—a quarter
moon cloud-ribbed high above the trees.

We didn't know how time would
change us, if anything might remain

the same—the essence of us still there,
phantoms of the old house, little apparitions

in whatever is left of the forest,
forever wandering the lost road home.

Like a Dream

Despite disappointments and detachments—four friends dead in just two years—the world hasn't stopped. Clocks keep ticking, the Pleiades stay in place (as if any of this were intended to last, as if we ever leave more than a spent breath of the soul blown through us).

And she knows how it feels, that wanting to go home. Like a dream (mostly peripheral), she calls back the murmured rustle of birds in trees; August nights filled with shooting stars; the way autumn dropped from the maple (wind-scrawled) in umber scrolls.

For her, it has always been the persuasion of twilight—how it falls in fractions, the way mist beads into dark—a soft voice, a brush of wings—the dream-relic feeling of time measured in moments.

No Such Thing

Last night I heard on TV that the Lady of the Lake
was an ancient astronaut, that she came from a
star in Orion's belt, or maybe Arcturus. After
that, I dreamt all night of arrows and swords.
Dream-queasy, somewhere between time and
tomorrow, a concave light inside the sky led me
along ley lines, and I hovered above Nazca, the
pyramids, Stonehenge—earthly reminders of what
we still don't know. Years ago, in a different dream,
an angel told me there's no such thing as disbelief.

The Way Things Are

It's the way things are. Banked in stillness,
distant trees notch the wind. A wild bird

hesitates between songs then flies into
sunset (a kind of shining). Afraid of losing

the earth and each other (whatever we're
here to do), we move closer—walk,

touch shoulders and hands, match our
footsteps in small subliminal rhythms.

In the last light, one cloud becomes a
mountain above the mountain. A flurry

of bats becomes the Milky Way, and we
make no pretense of understanding the

infinite, our need to become nothing
before we unname ourselves and disappear.

Even in This Splintered World

Because the Holy Ghost over the bent
World broods with warm breast and with ah! bright wings.
           (From "God's Grandeur" by Gerard Manley Hopkins)

I pray out here, in the shadow of the maple,
away from everything. Only in this detached
quiet am I able to silence the *I* in who I am—
another degree of second thought. The dog
I named for a poet is beside me—officially
Chaucer, I call him *Chaucey.* He's intuitive,
this one, as if he knows what I'm thinking

and thinks it with me. The cardinal pair is
here, two starlings, and a dove—all with
bright wings to lift them—and the red-bellied
woodpecker whose monophonic chant is
a rare form of apostolic blessing—nature's
Divine Office—its grace fundamental even
in this splintered world. I remember the night

you chanted "Dies Erae" at a poetry reading—
how, at the end, the whole room was so still
we all felt each other's heartbeats. *Believe,*
believe, I tell myself and, like a stuck song,
I inwardly quote Julian of Norwich over and
over—*All shall be well, and all shall be*
well, and all manner of thing shall be well.

II

~

*...the power of hoping through everything,
the knowledge that the soul survives its adventure,
that great inspiration comes to the middle-aged.*

—G. K. CHESTERTON

Whatever Else

This is the use of memory: / For liberation—not less of love but expanding / Of love beyond desire, and so liberation / From the future as well as the past.

(From "Little Gidding" by T.S. Eliot)

Who talks about *almost* or anything caught in a cleft of darkness—the deads' breath at the back of our necks? Whose voice do you almost hear when there's nothing to say? The rain, rattle-fisted (then) suddenly gone reminds us that nothing is permanent.

The gazebo in my garden begins to fall—squirrels have chewed through the screens, the roof is thin—something else to keep or let go. After so many years, I imagine its empty space and the wind that will blow through. This is the place where Eliot's rose garden meets the end of the world. I call each part of myself by name and live as if saving my life is the one thing I was made to do.

Distance and Now

Call it *back then* and know for sure that it stays.
Like blood, shed or dry, it lasts beyond the body—
a bird's wing that bends with the river and

continues into the sky. Never still or stiller, it
always unravels toward things that were
and will be. Somewhere on the other side

of distance and now, a man on the street
casts for clouds among serrated stars.
His tears fall like coins through a beggar's

hand. Mourners without knowing why (we
didn't ask for this), we think of tombstones
at our heads and try to feel what peace is like.

Then and What Happened

There were fingerprints on the nape of your neck, hands behind your eyes (eyes like stop—and oh, so brief). Have you forgotten: sweep and inner door, the sky arrow-boned and anxious—misgivings that came too late? I give you this: something ageless and undefined under sprawled stars—one night on the Via Sacra, in and through the Arch of Titus—an idea that slipped into consciousness; a circling bird with wings stretched farther than flight. And no words to string the air into music. Which of us wanted more, and what did loneliness mean except that summer was over?

What Yesterday Was

In the slanting drift of afternoon, even as
night begins to fall, our made-patterns of
thought and intention fade. The air lightens,
trees deepen, and a hermit thrush (distant

in the forest) invents songs that move through
the quiet. You haven't crossed my mind
in years, and I barely remember your face;
but, suddenly, here you are, the merest

recollection, shapeless as such remembrances
are—without substance or form—quickly
felt, then lost again. And what does such
fleeting memory stand for except that time

touches our hands and reminds us
(briefly) of whatever we meant to each
other, who we were and who we are—
what this day is, what yesterday was.

Among the Regrets

(After *Cloud Study* by John Constable, 1821)

It was how hills notched the sky's rim, the way clouds gathered behind the mountains—an old farmhouse, the white noise of wind on its roof, and a creek that rushed over stones and rose into mist like its own ghost; the flock of swallows that swept the sky like Constable's birds (careless and not).

She lifts a potted plant from the windowsill. Dusk slips in. The sky deepens into something darker, a shade of night she's never seen before. Shadows appear under the stars' weight like lingering dreams (and what came after). Among the regrets (all things impossible to keep)—a love that wasn't, but was.

Sheltered in Place (April 2020, Covid I)

April is the cruelest month, breeding
Lilacs out of the dead land

(From "The Waste Land" by T.S. Eliot)

I forget the date—13th, 14th—one number more than yesterday. There's a box of masks on the kitchen counter, a container of wipes under the sink. Local funeral homes rent freezer trucks to hold the dead. I think of the Monty Python movie—bodies piled into carts, the sound of wooden wheels on cobblestones—*Bring out your dead! Bring out your dead!* This might as well be the fourteenth century. My dreams are strange, filled with people and details I forgot years ago. One is recurrent—in it, a young girl flaps her arms like wings in crazy movements that clatter like stone birds. Her hands are dirty. Sometimes I see her blocks away, at the edge of a field, legs lost in nettles. She knows I'm unnerved, that I watch her, afraid that she's tracking me. When she stops in front of my house, I turn to the left and look down as if there's something to find between the garbage cans. A man walks his dog on the other side of the street. The dog lifts its leg on a neighbor's forsythia. Suddenly, the girl screams, her voice like numbers rising. The man pulls his dog away, walks around the corner and down Crest Lane. From the back, he looks like my father. Squirrels disappear into leaves; a chimney swift, high in a spiral of wind, is strung with the dust of a different light. Lilacs begin to bloom. In the end, we reclaim this world or leave it behind.

Another Week, Another Month (May 2020, Covid II)

The streets are empty, only a few cars in the train
station lot. Churches and synagogues are closed.
I read the same few pages two or three times before
I give up and put my book down. It's hard to concentrate,
impossible to center reflection, to find perspective.
My dog barks at the front door, but there's no one there.
He, too, is waiting. Neighborhood kids are strangely silent

as dusk turns into night / into day / into night. Another week,
another month. It seems ages since hyacinths bloomed and
their scent filled my yard in all directions like starlight.
Yesterday, a wren moved into the empty birdhouse. The
neighborhood woodchuck still comes around for apples,
things unchanged in her world while we (in masks and gloves)
continue distancing. I want to be where I was before,

with people who know me and people who don't. This is
neither the beginning of the story nor the end. And after
this time of uncertainty, what will define us? Resilience
and expectation? The cautious hope of a better world?
Tomorrow comes while we sleep but, right now, the way back
seems far too distant. I can't remember how it feels
to hug a friend, how it feels to shake a stranger's hand.

Remember (Ash Wednesday)

A robin (the first this year) stands where
tulips will open. Snowdrops bloom around the
fountain—new and sparkling in the still-cold
air. Sparrows and squirrels come to the feeding
table, wild but like old friends. After three years

of Covid, the news turned to Putin and, then
to Israel. Again, we watch cities leveled into
rubble and ash. We watch death happen.
History repeats and repeats—ashes to ashes.
Time and everything lost are ways of falling.

Here, a mockingbird sings another bird's song,
and I tell myself our human spirit is a springtime
that will go on rising until the sky turns and
takes us with it. I tell myself we are bits of sun
that glint like unexpected crystals on white stone.

The walk from one side of my fence to
the other is short. I pick up pine cones that
have fallen and bring them inside (like
all things essentially kept)—sometimes,
the best we can do is remember.

In Rain Like This

In rain like this, she always remembers the old house
and the mountains, how rain settled for days in the
hollow between two hills—without thunder, without

stopping. She remembers the way rain sounded then,
and deer in the forest, barely seen in spaces
between the trees. She remembers how rain raised the

creek and rushed it through the field's dim
glistening, the barn's slow ghost beneath the sky—
and all the words she meant to say but never did.

Elegy for the Man Who Collected Keys

He's out on a limb with tree bark under
his fingernails—again and against that
once real world—secrets strung from
star to star. It was the threat of sunset
and Professor Plum with a 22-caliber
book in the library. Everything is
metaphor. A branch's shadow swings
across the house; the statue he broke
has half a face. Dust burns into breath.
She stopped listening years ago.
Shoehorned in where he doesn't fit,
he has nothing to say.

The Man Who Is Last in Line

He looks at the people in front of him (everyone made of make believe). *There's only what the mirror thinks it sees,* he says. The others in line watch him watching them. Flies circle a greasy bag on the platform. He lifts one hand to his forehead, tips an imaginary hat in their direction, and looks out from under the brim. His coat is dirty, button holes frayed.

Loud in the cold, a train rumbles and chugs toward the end of its line. He takes a flattened penny from his pocket and flips it from hand to hand. Last week, he melted three gold chains in an iron crucible and molded them into a cross. Now, he stands between pigeons and dreams. The moon crouches and wavers. Brakes hiss and screech in the distance.

Stones Swung in Circles

It was weather for dreams;
for little fluttering quests of the heart.

(From *Dreamers* by Knut Hamsun)

I.

This isn't exactly the weather for dreams, but
here's one about a long drought and memories

of rain, the idea of connection and the way it
became air. In the unbalanced thought that

happens in dreams, it's never quite me doing
the thinking—not in any of them, especially

the ones that begin with ambiguous metaphors
and unresolved grief. I always look for the

presence in absence. But as soon as I hold
the moment, it turns away and is gone. In

this dream, it's Midsummer's Eve and
December at the same time. All night, snow

glaciers into mountains, and daylight (when
it comes) is so fierce it's frightening. Dawns

and sunsets whorl into backward and forward
motion then stop like overwound clocks.

The moon, in a fold of deepening sky, taps its
feet out of time, the sun shrinks and threatens

to disappear. Everything moves toward one
solstice or another—the calendar blurred.

II.

Another dream believes in heartbreak—always
less than and fewer—I remember it well

(wish you were here, wish I were there),
and the frozen loneliness of anything leaving.

In still another dream, the sky fills with a starling
mumuration—hundreds of birds, aligned in

direction and speed. They change the sky's surface
from tear drop forms to swirling batches of black—

trees in my yard overhung with thousands of wing
beats and flight calls. Music or noise, it's an exaltation

of some other language, a further occurrence of
words—an unsteady landscape I try to reshape.

Night into night, it's either heat-wilted peonies
or hydrangeas reduced to stalks encased in ice;

and one face that returns repeatedly among the
tens of others I've never bothered to name. Weathers

and dreams spiral like stones swung in circles
behind me. And (everything dropped from the sky

notwithstanding), this is about expectations of loss
and fluttering quests for things long passed

(some without record or designation) suspended
in a place that is neither illusion nor real.

No Longer Distracted

As if the columned clouds could change anything beneath the sky—she pretends not to notice as seasons change.

Just over her shoulder, she sees all the moons that have risen and set [since then]—her flannel shirt is frayed at the collar, blue jeans worn at the knees. Out of a two-dimensional sky, the sun rings its yellow bell. Inside, her hibiscus blooms—this morning three flowers on one stem (symbol and sign).

Birds that nested in her pocket disappear into winter's blanched monotony, and she looks down the staircase ahead. No longer distracted, she translates the long etceteras one step at a time— caught up in the actual *is*—the sudden presence, the open chord.

How Many Times

How many times did the woman impersonate herself—
the hummingbird's single note, her own wing spliced
through a needle's eye? Another glass of wine, another
repetition. Early this morning, she buried a squirrel that
died in her yard—dug the hole deeper than it needed to be
and held the small body close (still warm) until she
lowered it in (earth into body, body into earth)—
another hinge for the gate to swing on. For years,
she was everywhere she didn't want to be. Even in
the dark, she couldn't fall asleep until, finally,
with just enough rage, just enough grace—she
fit herself into a smaller life (free of history and
drama, free of every saint and insipid Hamlet)—
free of flesh, free of dust—the sky so skylessly blue.

What You Choose

You are here—by yourself—because that's
what you choose. Whether it's evening or
late afternoon (more dark, more light)
doesn't matter, the need to measure things
becomes less and less important. Strangely,

that doesn't surprise you. Lately, you think
how life rushes through everything—
unsettled dreams and things that will
never happen again. Above snow-melt
and bud, a weather vane turns (like old

lies—sharply directional—and you
wonder how long it will take to forgive
yourself). In a week or two, dogwoods
will float like watered silk across the
neighbor's yard. It's ironic that all your

seasons have led to reverence for things
that move slowly; how you, like anything
ordinary, changed without breaking.
A dog barks on the street behind you,
the sound distantly familiar. Language.

Landscape. In one of the trees, a small
bird sings—this one bird's one song
only for you because you are alone, and
you hear it the way you can almost hear
the time between breaths.

After It All

Sunlight sears one leaf and then another.
The fallen crackle underfoot. Octaves of wind
curve through pines where a redwing flashes
then disappears. Slowly, evening coils through
all the simplicities. I can't unsee what I've seen;
and so, yes, I've learned to justify choices,
and reimagine the afterworld into something
believable (as if, in my smallness, I might
illuminate the stars). In this conventional existence,
I know so little of ultimate reality (the mind's
true nature), and it doesn't matter that—*if*—
after it all, what I leave is little more than nothing.

III

࿔

Age has no reality except in the physical world.
The essence of a human being is resistant
to the passage of time. Our inner lives are eternal...

—GABRIEL GARCÍA MÁRQUEZ

This Moment

I

It's almost as if the catechism of earth
were written here, alchemized deep

in the grain of the poplars, in the
tongue-shaped leaves of the paper birch.

Today there are only tangled vines, a
worn footpath, and the unbroken peace

between us. High above, wild geese
veer and stretch toward the horizon,

their wings shaped to the wind. We pause
to watch them dissolve into specks on the

far side of the sky's wide curve. Circling,
a hawk lifts its shadow away from the

world, and I think to myself that a Power
we only begin to understand has called us

to this moment, this day, this place in time's
transept. Nothing happens by accident.

II

Far removed from the center of life, we
walk inside this borrowed hour, needing

only to be here, blessed by the quiet
confirmation that we've changed our lives.

It's almost winter, that acute emptiness,
which makes me see more intensely. The

wind remembers a greener season; cicada
shells crumble in the ivy. Time past and

present have become the same fixed minute
as sunlight slips behind the trees, and afternoon

darkens into a landscape where edges meet.
The hills lose shape. In this moment,

we credit the stars with revelation and hear
them singing. On the forest side, a half moon

crossed by branches rises in the vast and open
country where no one knows our names.

What Little We Know

No writing on the solitary, meditative dimensions of life
can say anything that has not already been said better
by the wind in the pine trees.
> (From *Love and Living* by Thomas Merton)

I haven't been here in such a long time,
I forgot how still the water is, how
soft the air—the quality of light as it

starts to fade. At dusk, the sky's cast
blue darkens and eddies gently toward
night. Close in the order of their being,

a deer and her fawn move away from
the forest to graze in a sheltered space
where field and woodland join.

Deep in the woods, tall pines fill with
wind that towers upward. It reminds
me that despite whatever falls, life

is still a skyward thing. It's good to
be alone with only these trees and
the wind—here in this other dimension.

Today is the Feast of Guardian Angels,
the ones who watch over and protect us.
Whether you believe in them or not,

such things seem possible here as
one bird scatters into dozens of smaller
birds that tip the sky forward before

they're gone—as we all must go,
taking with us what little we know of
infinite wisdom, infinite love.

Memory or Dream

Here, a Great Blue glides and dives;
a branch's shadow swings with birds.
Shadows filter through lines of pine, and
light flickers in the space between reality
and doubt. A feeling (almost remembered)
tells me I have been here before.

Above the tree line, a flock of starlings
skims through clouds and disappears.
Out of still water, moon-marbled and
clear as unseen air, a face I know looks
back at me with eyes that (in this life)
are mine, and studies me, measuring.

Into Night: At the Great Swamp

Gray on the path, my shadow
lengthens then disappears. Pitch Pines
edge into dusk. Here at the swamp,
twilight falls in degrees—first at
the sky's edge, into the treetops, and
then through underbrush on both sides
of a path edged with bracken and vines.
To the right of our car, a fox moves
through trees, into and out of focus.

Suddenly, a night bird rises, lifts
the water's sound, and becomes
the sky. Crickets and katydids churr.
Something small rustles in the
underbrush. I don't wonder where
love or the sun went, or why anything
else should matter but the startling
peace of this moment, the night's
long body, the stars' white fire.

And, Then,

For Laura Boss

It was over as suddenly as it began, a summer storm that swept in through heat and dense clouds—so brief it was almost momentary. You said it reminded you of life—here and, then, so quickly finished.

We sat in silence for a while before you asked if I believe in a life after this one. I told you I do, and you said you'd never been taught to believe in any life but this. You smiled a little sadly and asked if I could believe enough for both of us. Now, in the bleak reality of your death (this strange piece of night I try to see through), that conversation replays itself often.

Just before dawn this morning, I dreamt that you stood in a field with your parents. I knew who they were though I never met them or saw their pictures. Your son Jeffrey was with you and Michael (the man you loved for more than twenty years)— your puppies, Coco and Nelly, safe in your arms.

A small breeze crossed the field to touch my face—the warmth in that feeling as real as if this weren't a dream. Looking up, you smiled and, then, nodded toward me as if you were saying *yes.*

It's About

It's about what stays broken—
what she can't fix—her mother's pearls
(the fragile string in her hands), her
father's glasses (the splintering under
her foot). It's how everything that lasts
becomes holy—the way light shadows
a pine tree's branch, the garden's almost
sustainable brightness. It's about waiting
and what remains—each season's
subliminal rhythm, and the way she
holds her breath like a fistful of water.

Imagine a Dirt Path

Nothing changes the reality of things or the moon's upward arc. Nothing changes your cobbled soul, your fretted hands and the way memory staggers through them—the distance between you and yourself.

Imagine the dusk in you when the day turns back and retreats through spent leaves; imagine twilight's screen door and the way you close it behind you, the way your arm swings it shut; and then imagine a dirt path that leads through pine and cypress into something higher, a place where light moves into light.

What Happens

(After *The Glass Key*, by René Magritte)

[After that] first white of the deep snow, light of wonderment—
when you finally see it and almost know it for what it is: the
stone at the center of the stone, the flower at the center of the
flower.

On the front porch, an insect kisses the bug zapper and snaps
itself out of this world (gone like all the dead who wanted to
live—anonymous as moon moths and birdsong).

This is about whatever *spiritual* means and how it changes
us, how it makes us think deeply. It's what happens when we
reach a certain age and can look farther into the past than
we ever thought we would—the long backstory—it's when
we stand outside ourselves and begin to recognize our pre-
ordained smallness.

Before the Moon

Hers is the half world of a closed room
(striped curtains, scratched floorboards)
—something always missing, things
where they're not supposed to be. And now
summer—everything small against a wall

of heat—pine trees stooped at the garden's
edge. In this heat and this light (this trick
of light), finches fly from their unlikely nest
in the wreath above her door; dust burns
into breath. She doesn't know what to make

of herself, of anything broken. In these hot,
split days (stuck between spring and autumn),
she thinks about all that she can't hold,
what she can't keep—and how much more
she will have to let go. She thinks of the

moon (how, again and again, it thins and
fades), and she wonders how many ages
are left before it takes its last full turn
and rolls out of orbit, gone forever,
owing the world absolutely nothing.

And No One Knows

Most journeys begin on a ledge. She could
have jumped off, but prefers to remain unforgiven,
to slap dance on top of a dumpster (in time
with the wholeness of loss). Confess or
deny—intentions and sins are what's left.
Her Bible—that stop sign—lies on the dining
room table, vested in grief—and no one knows
what she feels when night falls and the horrors
come home. The argument is never about
acceptance; there is only the reach of things
that happen—the moments of life in between.

About Time Passing

She closes her eyes and the dark gets darker.
Fireflies and bottle caps flicker in the shadows.

One star fades above dark stones as clouds
move over it. She believes in the zero,

the transformation (some core of life after this
one); she believes in each year's turn around

the sun, and everything irreversible. Now, she
takes nothing for granted: the squirrels and

chipmunks, the birds that line up on her fence
each morning. There was never a touchstone

and no story more important than this. She tells
herself it's good enough to live with questions,

with the garden's chaplet of weeds, with all there
is—where everything is dear in this later light.

In Which the Sky

Blue jays screech above her house—a box on the stairs tips open (empty), but she never says *lonely*.

She loved a man once for the look of him and his hands (the way his knuckles whitened when he flicked cards against the fence), and his fingertips (stars that burned out long before she paused to look up). It was never about the all of him. In the end, he was just another lie that became the truth. The only thing she kept was his coat sleeve—the cuff shaped like disappointment.

She didn't foresee her father's death—years too soon—her mother's long illness and, then, the cancer diagnosis (twice) with her name in it. Forever after, light fell a little earlier, a little darker—so many things she never wanted to know.

They say time heals, and maybe it does. Shrugging, she says, *This is the way ghosts teach us*. Above the distant rumble of jack-hammers and thunder, the sky crests like a wave as she pulls it in behind her.

Where Eternity Is Learned

For Alex Pinto

First the high hedge turns with birds that
vanish into wings. Trees darken before

the sky; the field that was once a forest
loses dimension. Change is a meshed idea

that filters through our bodied lives.
Once, we back-viewed our dead together,

took our seats in a new front row, and
bowed to the god of collapsed possibilities—

god of fragments, god of the past imperfect—
whatever magic was left. Completely

unprepared for what would come,
I never thought: no retrieval, no return.

And you, fallen into a brace of echoes—
memories already beginning to diminish.

With no debt to the future, I live in the
pure constant of what each moment is.

Bent tightly into the dim underwood
of my own bonescape, I look to a point

where the world goes on without me,
to the place where eternity is learned.

If Not Happiness Itself

In the twilight of life (this here and this
now), my Yorkshire Terrier sleeps on
the bench beside me. To our right are
the blue angel hosta and a pink tea rose
that blooms against the garden fence—
here are the moment and memory of
hummingbirds in the bee balm, a

goldfinch in the thistle. The mockingbird
that tamed itself takes a peanut from
my hand. Among the losses and all
the regrets, this small, gray bird appeared
one day and stayed. Every morning,
it waits for me to come outside, and it
sings to the difference between absence

and presence, to all the odds and ends
of life that call me now to something
peaceful (if not happiness itself), something
that's not about what's happened or what
happens next. In this here and this now,
the past fits into its own back pocket—
ready for me to carry home.

What There Is Instead

It's what happens when the *almosts* and the *what ifs* became a hallway too long to look down. It's when wintering can't be broad-brushed away. For now, we are here—the sky spread with stars transfixed on their stems like vacant lovers.

Once we were young and filled with plans—we did what we wanted to do, what we *could* do—before we became what life made us. There was no foretelling and nothing promised—no way to know what might be certain (what would stay, what would disappear).

A flicker drills its version of words into a distant tree. Somewhere infinity meets a shoreline. Night falls with all of its silences; and, finally, it's okay to think beyond this world, beyond ourselves. It's okay to not know, to wonder what there is instead.

The Moonlight You Were

*Once you have have tasted flight you will forever walk the earth
with your eyes turned skyward, for there you have been and there
you will always long to return.*
   (From the film *I, Leonardo da Vinci* by John Hermes Secondari)

Imagine for a moment that you hadn't stumbled through
summer, that you hadn't thrown rocks at the sun; and winter,
when it came out of turn, hadn't changed you. Imagine that
things don't have to make sense—things like *why*, and the light
of another time that walks behind you.

You cast your shadow back into yourself, and your revenants,
returned into being, appear without invitation. Their wings
remember the victory of flight—as if to confirm death's
impermanence.

Imagine, then, that you become the moonlight you were. That
you've walked past the rough country of everywhere else you've
been. A stream in front of you flows slowly, and your hand
reaches forward to touch the sky.

More to Consider

Still the intimate outsider, made up of make believe in a place
where everything changes—she knows that no end is ever cho-
sen by its beginning. A stack of books lies on the garden bench;
birds watch from the trees—sparrows and one gray dove. A
flick of moon rises above (flutter and wing away). There's so
much more to consider than the weight of risk or endurance:
what belongs where, and what backup will be in place when
all else fails. She's still working out what happens between love
and forgiveness, where the ancient energies converge, their one
source. So many approaches to the promise—like faith, the
power of the idea—she still believes that everything is sacred.

Acknowledgments

Grateful acknowledgment is made to the editors and publishers of the following journals and anthologies in which poems from this collection have appeared or are forthcoming (some in earlier forms and with earlier titles):

Adanna—"Before the Moon" and "Anything with Wings"

Edison Literary Review—"Time Warp" and "Another Week, Another Month"

Exit 13—"What Little We Know" (under an earlier title) and "If Not Happiness Itself"

Frost Meadow Review (Pandemic Poetry)—"Even in this Splintered World" (revised sections of the original poem, "All Manner of Thing," are included in this new version)

Invasion of the Ukraine 2022 (curated online by Richard Levine and Michael T. Young for Djelloul Marbrook's *PRISM*)—"Remember"

Lips Poetry Journal—"That Little While…," "Remember" (under an earlier title), "And, Then," "What Happens," "More to Consider," "What You Choose" (also in *Wind Over Stones*, an earlier version, under a different title), and "What There Is Instead"

Lothlorien Poetry Journal—"Exactly Then"

MacQueen's Quinterly—"Then and What Happened"

New Jersey Bards Poetry Review 2023—"Like a Dream"

New Jersey Bards Poetry Review 2024—"What Little We Know"

Orenaug Mountain Poetry Journal—"Into Night"

The Doll Collection (Diane Lockward, Editor), Terrapin Books—"Of Shadows" (originally published in an earlier version under a different title)

The Night Heron Barks—"Whatever Else"

The Orchards Poetry Journal—"More to Consider"

Paterson Literary Review—"One of Us" and "Things You're Told"

The Pedestal—"In Which the Sky"

The Raven's Perch—"On Summer Nights," "What Yesterday Was," and "It's About"

Shot Glass Journal—"No Such Thing" and "And No One Knows"

The Silence and the Flame and *Chosen Ghosts*—Sections of "This Moment" appeared in separate poems, in early versions, under different titles.

Stillwater Review—"In Rain Like This," "Memory or Dream," "Into Night: At the Great Swamp," "The Way Things Are" (also in *Wind Over Stones,* an earlier version, under a different title), and "Even in This Splintered World"

The Strategic Poet (Diane Lockward, Editor), Terrapin Books—"The Old House"

SurVision—"How Many Times" and "Elegy for the Man Who Collected Keys"

This Broken Shore, 2020, 2021, 2022, and *2024* (Dan Weeks, Editor, Coleridge Institute Press)—"Distance and Now," "Imagine a Dirt Path" (in an earlier version, under a different title), "The Moonlight You Were," and "The Way Things Are"

Tiferet—"Sheltered in Place"

U.S. 1 Worksheets—"Among the Regrets," "About Time Passing," and "After It All"

Verse Daily—"Time Warp" and "Another Week, Another Month"

What the House Knows (Diane Lockward, Editor), Terrapin Books—"Anything with Wings"

Additional Acknowledgments

"One of Us" received the first prize Allen Ginsberg Poetry Award (2021).

"That Little While" (*Lips Poetry Journal*) and "If Not Happiness Itself" (*Exit 13*) received Pushcart Prize Nominations.

"And No One Knows" was nominated for the Best of the Net (*Shot Glass Journal*)

Special thanks to my publisher, John Weber, for being (without exception) the best; to Nancy Lubarsky, Tom Plante, and Bob Rosenbloom—my poetry buddies—for so many years of support and encouragement; to Bob Fiorellino for always being there; to my Yorkshire Terrier, Chaucer, who's never far from my side; and to Charles DeFanti for nearly sixty years of unfailing friendship and guidance.

About the Author

Adele Kenny, founding director of the Carriage House Poetry Series (1998-present) and poetry editor of *Tiferet Journal* (2006-present), is a poet and nonfiction writer. Her poems, reviews, and articles have been widely published in the U.S. and abroad, and her poems have appeared in books and anthologies from Crown, Tuttle, Shambhala, and McGraw-Hill. She is the recipient of various awards, including two poetry fellowships from the NJ State Arts Council, various agency-sponsored writing grants, a Union County Freeholders H.E.A.R.T. grant, a first place Allen Ginsberg Poetry Award, a Merton Poetry of the Sacred Award, a Women of Excellence Award (Union County Commission on the Status of Women, for achievements and volunteer work in the arts and humanities), and Kean University's Distinguished Alumni Award. Her book *A Lightness, a Thirst, or Nothing at All* was a Paterson Poetry Prize finalist. She has also won numerous awards for her haiku, including a first place Merit Book Award, first place Henderson Award, first place Raymond Roseliep Memorial Award, first place Renku Award, first place Haiku Quarterly Award, Museum of Haiku Literature Awards, a Tiny Poems Press Award, and one of her haiku appeared on the marquee of the Rialto West Theater (NYC) as part of the 42nd Street Art Project. A former creative writing professor in the College of New Rochelle's Graduate School, she also taught report writing at the John H. Stamler Police Academy. Poet Laureate of Fanwood, NJ since 2012, she has read her poetry in the U.S., England, France, and Ireland, and has twice been a Geraldine R. Dodge Festival poet.

Website: www.adelekenny.com